Penguins
And Their Young

Teacher's Guide

Preschool–1

Skills
Observing, Comparing,
Communicating, Creative and
Logical Thinking, Role Playing

Concepts
Penguin Habitat, Body Structure, Parenting,
Feeding Strategies, Heat and Warmth,
Melting, Freezing, Ice, Floating, Size, Shape

Themes
Patterns of Change, Scale,
Structure, Energy, Systems and
Interactions, Diversity and Unity,
Models and Simulations
(For more about **Themes**, see page 71)

Math Strands
Measurement, Number, Pattern, Logic

by
Jean C. Echols

GEMS
Great Explorations in Math and Science
Lawrence Hall of Science
University of California at Berkeley

LHS GEMS

Lawrence Hall of Science
　　Chairman: Glenn T. Seaborg
　　Director: Marian C. Diamond

Initial support for the origination and publication of the GEMS series was provided by the A.W. Mellon Foundation and the Carnegie Corporation of New York. GEMS has also received support from the McDonnell-Douglas Foundation and the McDonnell-Douglas Employees Community Fund, the Hewlett Packard Company Foundation, and the people at Chevron USA. GEMS also gratefully acknowledges the contribution of word processing equipment from Apple Computer, Inc. This support does not imply responsibility for statements or views expressed in publications of the GEMS program.

Under a grant from the National Science Foundation, GEMS Leader's Workshops have been held across the country. For further information on GEMS leadership opportunities, or to receive a publication brochure and the *GEMS Network News*, please contact GEMS at the address and phone number provided.

Development of this guide was sponsored in part by a grant from the National Science Foundation.

COMMENTS WELCOME

Great Explorations in Math and Science (GEMS) is an ongoing curriculum development project. GEMS guides are revised periodically, to incorporate teacher comments and new approaches. We welcome your criticisms, suggestions, helpful hints, and any anecdotes about your experience presenting GEMS activities. Your suggestions will be reviewed each time a GEMS guide is revised. Please send your comments to:

　　GEMS Revisions
　　Lawrence Hall of Science
　　University of California
　　Berkeley, CA 94720-5200

Our phone number is (510) 642-7771.
Our fax number is (510) 643-0309.

STAFF

Principal Investigator
Glenn T. Seaborg
Director
Jacqueline Barber
Assistant Director
Kimi Hosoume
Curriculum Specialist
Cary Sneider
GEMS Centers Coordinator
Carolyn Willard
GEMS Workshop Coordinator
Laura Tucker
GEMS Workshop Representative
Terry Cort
Staff Development Specialists
Katharine Barrett, John Erickson,
Jaine Kopp, Laura Lowell, Linda Lipner
Mathematics Consultant
Jan M. Goodman
Administrative Coordinator
Cynthia Eaton
Distribution Coordinator
Karen Milligan
Shipping Coordinator
Felicia Roston
Shipping Assistant
George Kasarjian
Program Assistant
Stephanie Van Meter
Principal Editor
Lincoln Bergman
Senior Editor
Carl Babcock
Assistant Editor
Florence Stone
Principal Publications Coordinator
Kay Fairwell
Art Director
Lisa Haderlie Baker
Designers
Carol Bevilacqua, Rose Craig, Lisa Klofkorn
Staff Assistants
Larry Gates, Alisa Sramala, Mary Yang

Great Explorations in Math and Science (GEMS) Program

The Lawrence Hall of Science (LHS) is a public science center on the University of California at Berkeley campus. LHS offers a full program of activities for the public, including workshops and classes, exhibits, films, lectures, and special events. LHS is also a center for teacher education and curriculum research and development.

Over the years, LHS staff have developed a multitude of activities, assembly programs, classes, and interactive exhibits. These programs have proven to be successful at the Hall and should be useful to schools, other science centers, museums, and community groups. A number of these guided-discovery activities have been published under the Great Explorations in Math and Science (GEMS) title, after an extensive refinement process that includes classroom testing of trial versions, modifications to ensure the use of easy-to-obtain materials, and carefully written and edited step-by-step instructions and background information to allow presentation by teachers without special background in mathematics or science.

Contributing Authors

Jacqueline Barber
Katharine Barrett
Lincoln Bergman
Ellen Blinderman
Beatrice Boffen
Celia Cuomo
Linda De Lucchi
Jean Echols
John Erickson
Jan M. Goodman
Alan Gould
Debra Harper
Kimi Hosoume
Sue Jagoda
Jaine Kopp
Linda Lipner
Laura Lowell
Larry Malone
Cary I. Sneider
Jennifer Meux White
Carolyn Willard

PEACHES

ACKNOWLEDGMENTS

Photographs: Richard Hoyt
Illustrations and Poster: Rose Craig
Cover: Lisa Haderlie Baker

Thanks to all the enthusiastic people on the PEACHES committee at the Lawrence Hall of Science—Katharine Barrett, Ellen Blinderman, Beatrice Boffen, Jean Echols, Kay Fairwell, Kimi Hosoume, Jaine Kopp, Bernadette Lauraya, and Jennifer Meux White—for their many suggestions and other contributions during the development and writing of *Penguins And Their Young*. Special thanks go to Kimi Hosoume for her help during the final writing of this guide and to Jaine Kopp for writing the Hungry Penguins Game, inspired by the Whale Game in *Mathematics Their Way* by Mary Baratta-Lorton.

We want to especially thank teachers Pamela Curtis-Horton of Emerson Elementary School and Karen Fong of Sequoia Nursery School in Oakland, California, for the generous gift of their time in helping us photograph the *Penguins And Their Young* activities. And thanks go to all the children in their classes who enlivened the photographs in this guide.

REVIEWERS

We would like to thank the following educators who reviewed, tested, or coordinated the reviewing of *this series* of GEMS/PEACHES materials in manuscript and draft form. Their critical comments and recommendations, based on presentation of these activities nationwide, contributed significantly to these GEMS publications. Their participation in the review process does not necessarily imply endorsement of the GEMS program or responsibility for statements or views expressed. Their role is an invaluable one, and their feedback is carefully recorded and integrated as appropriate into the publications.

ALASKA

Coordinator: **Cynthia Dolmas Curran**

Creative Play Preschool, Wasilla
Ronda Ingham
Mary Percak-Dennett

Iditarod Elementary School, Wasilla
Beverly McPeek

Wasilla Middle School, Wasilla
Cynthia Dolmas Curran

ARIZONA

Coordinator: **Mary Jo Eckhardt**

Julia Randall Elementary School, Payson
Mary Jo Eckhardt
Terri Legassie
Kay Wilson

Payson Head Start, Payson
Dani Rosenstell

CALIFORNIA

Coordinators: **Kathy Moran, Floria Spencer, Rebecca Wheat, Dottie Wiggins**

4C's Children's Center, Oakland
Yolanda Coleman-Wilson

24 Hour Children Center, Oakland
Sheryl Lambert
Ella Tassin
Inez Watson

Afterschool Program, Piedmont
Willy Chen

Alameda Head Start, Alameda
Michelle Garabedian
Debbie Garcia
Stephanie Josey

Albany Children's Center, Albany
Celestine Whittaker

Bancroft School, Berkeley
Cecilia Saffarian

Bartell Childcare and Learning Center, Oakland
Beverly Barrow
Barbara Terrell

Beach Elementary School, Piedmont
Ann Blasius
Juanita Forester
Elodee Lessley
Jean Martin

Belle Vista Child Development Center, Oakland
Satinder Jit K. Rana

Berkeley-Albany YMCA, Berkeley
Trinidad Caselis

Berkeley Hills Nursery School, Berkeley
Elizabeth Fulton

Berkeley/Richmond Jewish Community, Berkeley
Terry Amgott-Kwan

Berkeley Unified School District, Berkeley
Rebecca Wheat

Berkwood-Hedge School, Berkeley
Elizabeth Wilson

Bernice & Joe Play School, Oakland
Bernice Huisman-Humbert

Bing School, Stanford
Kate Ashbey

Brookfield Elementary School, Oakland
Kathy Hagerty
Linda Rogers

Brookfield Head Start, Oakland
Suzie Ashley

Butte Kiddie Corral, Shingletown
Cindy Stinar Black

Cedar Creek Montessori, Berkeley
Idalina Cruz
Jeanne Devin
Len Paterson

Centro Vida, Berkeley
Rosalia Wilkins

Chinese Community United Methodist Church, Oakland
Stella Ko Kwok

Clayton Valley Parent Preschool, Concord
Lee Ann Sanders
Patsy Sherman

Compañeros del Barrio State Preschool, San Francisco
Anastasia Decaristos
Laura Todd

Contra Costa College, San Pablo
Sylvia Alvarez-Mazzi

Creative Learning Center, Danville
Brooke H. B. D'Arezzo

Creative Play Center, Pleasant Hill
Debbie Coyle
Sharon Keane

Dena's Day Care, Oakland
Kawsar Elshinawy

Dover Preschool, Richmond
Alice J. Romero

Duck's Nest Preschool, Berkeley
Pierrette Allison
Patricia Foster
Mara Ellen Guckian
Ruth Major

East Bay Community Children's Center, Oakland
Charlotte Johnson
Oletha R. Wade

Ecole Bilingue, Berkeley
Nichelle R. Kitt
Richard Mermis
Martha Ann Reed

Emerson Child Development Center, Oakland
Ron Benbow
Faye McCurtis
Vicky Wills

Emerson Elementary School, Oakland
Pamela Curtis-Horton

Emeryville Child Development Center, Emeryville
Ellastine Blalock
Jonetta Bradford
Ortencia A. Hoopii

Enrichment Plus Albert Chabot School, Oakland
Lisa Dobbs

Family Day Care, Oakland
Cheryl Birden
Penelope Brody
Eufemia Buena Byrd
Mary Waddington

Family Day Care, Orinda
Lucy Inouye

Gan Hillel Nursery School, Richmond
Denise Moyes-Schnur

Gan Shalom Preschool, Berkeley
Iris Greenbaum

Garner Toddler Center, Alameda
Uma Srinath

Gay Austin, Albany
Sallie Hanna-Rhyne

Giggles Family Day Care, Oakland
Doris Wührmann

Greater Richmond Social Services Corp., Richmond
Lucy Coleman

Happy Lion School, Pinole
Sharon Espinoza
Marilyn Klemm

Hintil Kuu Ca Child Development Center, Oakland
Eunice C. Blago
Kathy Moran
Gina Silber
Agnes Tso
Ed Willie

Jack-in-the-Box Junction Preschool, Richmond
Virginia Guadarrama

Kinder Care, Oakland
Terry Saugstad

King Child Development Center, Berkeley
Joan Carr
Diane Chan
Frances Stephens
Eula Webster
Dottie Wiggins

King Preschool, Richmond
Charlie M. Allums

The Lake School, Oakland
Margaret Engel
Patricia House
Vickie Stoller

Learning Adventures Child Development, Redding
Dena Keown

Longfellow Child Development Center, Oakland
Katryna Ray

Los Medanos Community College, Pittsburg
Judy Henry
Filomena Macedo

Maraya's Developmental Center, Oakland
Maria A. Johnson-Price
Gayla Lucero

Mark Twain School Migrant Education, Modesto
Grace Avila

Mary Jane's Preschool, Pleasant Hill
Theresa Borges

Merritt College Children's Center, Oakland
Deborah Green
Virginia Shelton

Mickelson's Child Care, Ramona
Levata Mickelson

Mills College Children's Center
Monica Grycz

Mission Head Start, San Francisco
Pilar Marroquin
Mirna Torres

The Model School Comprehensive, Berkeley
Jenny Schwartz-Groody

Montclair Community Play Center, Oakland
Elaine Guttmann
Nancy Kliszewski
Mary Loeser

Next Best Thing, Oakland
Denise Hingle
Franny Minervini-Zick

Oak Center Christian Academy, Oakland
Debra Booze

Oakland Parent Child Center, Oakland
Barbara Jean Jackson

Oakland Unified School District, Oakland
Floria Spencer

Orinda Preschool, Orinda
Tracy Johansing-Spittler

Oxford St. Learning Road, Berkeley
Vanna Maria Kalofonos

Peixoto Children's Center, Hayward
Alma Arias
Irma Guzman
Paula Lawrence
Tyra Toney

Piedmont Cooperative Playschool, Piedmont
Marcia Nybakken

Playmates Daycare, Berkeley
Mary T. McCormick

Rainbow School, Oakland
Mary McCon
Rita Neely

REVIEWERS

San Antonio Head Start, Oakland
Cynthia Hammock
Ilda Terrazas

San Jose City College, San Jose
Mary Conroy

Sequoia Nursery School, Oakland
Karen Fong
Lorraine Holmstedt

Sequoyah Community Preschool, Oakland
Erin Smith
Kim Wilcox

Shakelford Head Start, Modesto
Teresa Avila

So Big Preschool, Antioch
Linda Kochly

St. Vincent's Day Home, Oakland
Pamela Meredith

Sunshine Preschool, Berkeley
Poppy Richie

U. C. Berkeley Child Care Services
Smyth Fernwald II, Berkeley
Diane Wallace
Caroline W. Yee

Walnut Ave. Community Preschool, Walnut Creek
Evelyn DeLanis

Washington Child Development Center, Berkeley
Reather Jones

Washington Kids Club, Berkeley
Adwoa A. Mante

Westview Children's Center, Pacifica
Adrienne J. Schneider

Woodroe Woods, Hayward
Wendy Justice

Woodstock Child Development Center, Alameda
Mary Raabe
Denise M. Ratto

Woodstock School, Alameda
Amber D. Cupples

Yuk Yan Annex, Oakland
Eileen Lok

YWCA Oakland, Oakland
Iris Ezeb
Grace Perry

MISSISSIPPI
Coordinator: **Josephine Gregory**

Little Village Child Development Center, Jackson
Josephine Gregory
Patrick Gregory
Denise Harris
Barbara Johnson

NEW YORK
Coordinators: **Stephen Levey, Mary Jean Syrek**

Aquarium for Wildlife Conservation, Brooklyn
Meryl Kafka

Dr. Charles R. Drew Science Magnet, Buffalo
Linda Edwards
Carol Podger
Diana Roberts
Willie Robinson
Mary Jean Syrek

PS 329—Surfside School, Brooklyn
Sharon Fine
Valerie LaManna
Stephen Levey
Barbara Nappo
Angela Natale
Arline Reisman

TEXAS
Coordinator: **Myra Luciano**

Armand Bayou Elementary School, Houston
Myra Luciano

John F. Ward Elementary School, Houston
Brenad Greenshields
Luanne Lamar
Vicki Peterson
Jenny Scott

WASHINGTON
Coordinator: **Peggy Willcuts**

Blue Ridge Mountain School, Walla Walla
Elizabeth Arebalos
Sandi Burt
Gail Callahan
Leah Crudup
Peggy Willicuts

CONTENTS

GEMS and PEACHES

GEMS is publishing a number of early childhood activity guides developed by the PEACHES project of the Lawrence Hall of Science. PEACHES is a curriculum development and training program for teachers and parents of children in preschool through first grade.

Like the GEMS guides already available for preschool and the early grades—such as *Hide A Butterfly*, *Animal Defenses*, and *Buzzing A Hive*—the new PEACHES guides combine free exploration, drama, art, and literature with science and mathematics to give young children positive and effective learning experiences.

Introduction

Many children are fascinated by penguins, maybe because this comical, black and white bird seems like one of them. It stands upright as they do and it can be as tall as many preschoolers. *Penguins And Their Young* features the emperor penguin, the tallest of the penguins. Youngsters learn about its body structure, its cold home of ice and water, what it eats, and how emperor penguin parents take care of their young.

Life science, math, and physical science are tightly integrated with language development in this unit. The children have fun learning through drama, role playing, and creative play as well as by observing and comparing icy shapes in water. This approach creates enthusiasm in children and motivates them to learn in all areas of the curriculum.

Learning Life Science through Drama, Play, and Role Play

The children learn about penguin body structure by making paper-bag penguins, which they use in a drama about parent penguins caring for their eggs and young during the very cold and windy winter months. Parents and teachers join the children in role-playing penguins waddling around on the ice or holding eggs on their feet to keep the eggs warm. As the children play with their penguins and role-play penguins, they often recall and act out real penguin behavior.

Learning Math through Comparisons and Role Play

Measurement and number activities relate penguin size and behaviors to those of young children. The children compare their heights with the height of the emperor penguin and their hands and feet with the size of the emperor's egg and chick. In the Hungry Penguins Game, the girls and boys listen to a story about fish and penguins swimming in the ocean. Pretending they are hungry penguins, youngsters add and take away (by eating) fish crackers on blue paper oceans. While playing this game, the children practice problem solving, counting, one-to-one correspondence, addition, and subtraction.

Learning Physical Science through Creative Play

Floating, freezing, and melting are a few of the physical science concepts introduced during these ice and water activities. The children first play freely with water, ice, cork penguins, and toy fish. When the youngsters create colored ice shaped like hands, balloons, and shells, they discover ice can have many shapes, textures, and colors. Playing with ice leads to doing simple

Penguin deluxe,
Bird in a tux,
Elegant, debonair.
Birds of a feather
Who *do* flock together
But never take to the air!

— *Lincoln Bergman*

investigations with melting ice, in which the youngsters follow the process of guessing what may happen to the ice, and then observing and discussing what did happen.

Developing Language through Play, Drama, and Role Play

After playing with their paper penguins, watching The Penguin Drama, and role-playing penguins, the boys and girls become so involved with penguins that they are excited about sharing their ideas and creating their own penguin stories and dramas. They are eager to listen to penguin stories, and write down or tell interesting facts about penguins. They draw and paint pictures of penguins to illustrate their stories.

Activities for a Wide Range of Abilities

Although the activities in *Penguins And Their Young* are for children in preschool through first grade, they can be adapted upward for second and third graders. Because of a wide range of abilities, some of the activities are more appropriate for younger children and others for older students. It is not necessary to do every activity with each age group.

For preschoolers, keep the activities short and introduce only a few concepts, facts, and new words in each session. Take advan-

tage of every opportunity for role playing. The younger the children the more they enjoy waddling and "sliding" on their bellies like penguins. Older children can handle more discussion and more detailed observations.

The lesson descriptions include suggestions for modifying the activities to make them appropriate for the level of your students. Extensions for First Graders, placed at the end of some sections, suggests ways to extend the activities for older students.

Suggestions for Using This Book

- Some of the sessions in this book are short, but can be combined with other sessions. The "Going Further" sections have suggestions for activities to extend the sessions. If you choose to do these, they can be done on another day.

- Most of the activities in this book can be done in small groups or stations. Several days in advance, arrange for adults or older students to help with activities such as the ice explorations, body tracings, and filling balloons with water. The Penguin Drama and the role playing usually work well with the whole class.

- Often we include questions to ask the children. Many of these questions are open-ended and encourage the children to come up with their own ideas. Their answers give you insight into their thinking. All responses from the children should be recognized in a positive way. In this book, possible answers to the questions are included after the question in brackets [brackets]. These responses are some of the answers you might expect from your children. They are not meant to be used to correct the children or to give them the "right" answer. The bracketed answers are provided as a reference for you to better clarify the information being addressed.

- The full-page illustrations in the book are given again at the back of the book and perforated so you can tear them out for easy duplication.

- If you are working with children too young to use scissors, you can do any necessary cutouts beforehand and have the materials ready for the children's activity.

- On page 57 are "Summary Outlines" of all the activities, which you can use as a quick reminder when you present the activities.

- As you present the activities, you may wish to refer to the "Literature Connections" on page 55, which annotate children's literature that contains themes and situations relevant to a particular activity. These books could be read aloud during that activity.

Activity 1: A Home of Ice and Water

Overview

The stage is set for learning about penguins and their cold home of ice and water. The children watch water freeze and ice melt, and play with floating ice, cork penguins, and toy fish in a pan of water. The boys and girls compare their height with a life-size drawing of an emperor penguin to find out whether they are taller or shorter than the penguin.

For preschoolers, the process of watching water turn into ice is an exciting learning experience. If you work with older children who are very familiar with this process, you may decide to begin Activity 1 with Session 2 and bring ice to class.

As the youngsters observe the ice, an enthusiastic child may say, "Look, the ice is getting smaller and smaller" or "This water is turning cold because there's a big chunk of ice in it." These activities provide opportunities for you to observe how the children learn while playing freely with the ice and other materials.

Session 1: From Water to Ice

What You Need

For the whole group
- ❏ 1 freezer, large enough to hold the milk carton(s) and cups (see below)
- ❏ 1 waterproof black marking pen
- ❏ 1 sturdy, waterproof tray for every 8–12 children

For each group of four children
- ❏ 1 large dishpan about 20" x 15" x 5", or use a water table
- ❏ 1 empty half-gallon milk carton, or 1 loaf pan
- ❏ 1 towel

For each child
- ❏ 1 small plastic cup (3–8 oz.)
optional
  - ❏ 1 change of clothing

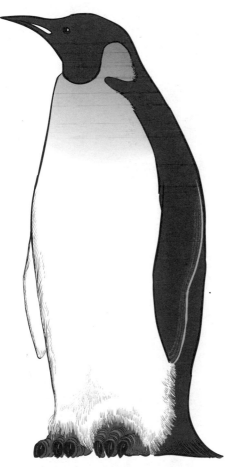

Emperor Penguin

Getting Ready

Anytime Before the Activity

Plan to start this activity when the children first arrive so they will have time to see the water begin to freeze.

Several Days Before the Activity

1. Arrange for adult help to supervise small groups of children.

2. Make room for the milk cartons and cups in your freezer.

Immediately Before the Activity

1. Fill one dishpan with water for each group of four children. If the weather is warm and sunny, place the pans outside.

2. Use the waterproof pen to write a child's name on each cup.

Water

1. Have four children gather around each pan of water.

2. Give each child a cup with his or her name on it. Let the children spend as much time as they like playing with the cups in the water.

3. Put an empty milk carton in each pan of water, and let each group play in the water with the cups and carton.

Water Into Ice

1. While the children are watching, fill a milk carton with water and ask, "What do you think will happen to the water if we put it in the freezer?" Fill a milk carton for each small group, and put the cartons on the tray.

2. Let each child fill their cup with water and put the cup on the tray.

3. If possible, let the children watch as you carry the tray to the freezer and put the cups and milk cartons inside.

4. With the children, check the water several times throughout the day to find out what is happening to the water.

5. Leave the milk cartons and cups in the freezer until the water is frozen. You will use the ice in the next activity.

If you don't have a freezer at school, freeze the ice at home and bring it to school in an ice chest.

We find when filling the dishpans with water—because of the weight— it is easiest to partially fill them at the sink and finish filling them at the table.

If you have limited space, put as many cups and cartons as you can in the freezer. When the water is frozen, stack the cups and milk cartons, and add more. Keep freezing and stacking until you have enough ice for your class.

Session 2: An Ice Home

What You Need

For the whole group

❏ 1 Emperor Penguin poster

optional

❏ 1 black waterproof marking pen, or black crayon

❏ 1 ice chest (If there is no freezer you can use at school, make the ice at home and take it to school in an ice chest. An ice chest is also useful if the school freezer is far from your classroom.)

❏ Pictures of animals that live on ice, such as polar bears, seals, and walruses

For each group of four children

❏ 1 large dishpan about 20" x 15" x 5", or use a water table

❏ 1 block of ice in a half-gallon milk carton, or loaf pan (from Session 1)

❏ 1 towel

For each child

❏ 1 cork about 2" high

❏ 1 plastic fish about 1" long

❏ 1 chunk of ice in a small plastic cup (from Session 1)

optional

❏ 1 change of clothing

❏ 1 black crayon

Instead of corks, some teachers use 2"–4" plastic penguins.

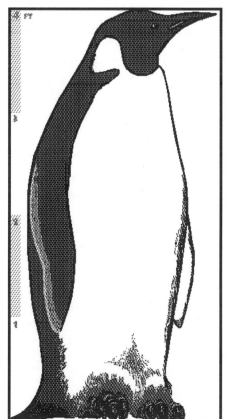

Getting Ready

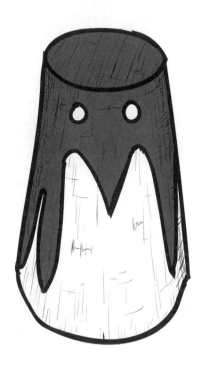

Anytime Before the Activity

Optional

    If you use corks for penguins, use the waterproof pen or crayon to draw penguin features on the corks. (See the drawing on this page.) First grade students can use crayons to draw features on their own cork penguins. Please note that the crayon may leave marks on the dishpan when the children "dive" their penguins to the bottom.

Several Days Before the Activity

Arrange for adult help to supervise small groups of children.

Immediately Before the Activity

1. Fill one dishpan with cool water for each group of four children.

2. Take the milk cartons out of the freezer about 15 minutes before you begin the section Making a Home for Penguins on page 10.

Getting to Know Penguins

1. Gather the children in a half circle on the floor. Tell the group that some animals live on the ice. Ask, "What animals can you think of that live on ice?"

    Optional

    Show pictures of the animals as the children name them.

2. Say, "I am thinking of an animal that is black and white and lives on the ice. What is it?" If the children don't guess, give them a hint by waddling and shuffling around like a penguin.

3. Show the Emperor Penguin poster to the group and ask, "What animal is this?"

4. Ask questions that encourage the children to talk about penguins, such as:
   - Have you ever seen a real penguin?
   - Where did you see it?
   - What was it doing?
   - What do you like about penguins?

5. Have a child point to the penguin's wings. Tell the children that a penguin is a bird that does not fly. Ask, "What do you think it does with its wings?" [swims]

6. Ask, "How do you think it moves on the ice?" [walks, waddles, slides, shuffles] If the children don't already know, tell them that penguins also slide on their bellies on the ice.

Ice and Water

1. Take the children with you to remove their cups from the freezer or ice chest.

2. Give each child his or her cup. Ask, "What happened to the water?"

3. Gather the children in a half circle on the floor, and let them examine the ice by touching and smelling it.

4. Ask questions about the ice, such as:
   - What does the ice look like?
   - Do you see anything in the ice? [bubbles, lines]
   - How does it feel?

5. Encourage the children to share their observations. A child may comment, "The cup is cold" or "There's ice on the outside of the cup."

6. If a child says the ice is melting ask, "What happens to the ice when it melts?" [It turns to water. It gets smaller.] With kindergarten and first grade children ask, "Why do you think the ice is melting?"
   When you ask a thoughtful question, the children have a chance to come up with their own ideas. Their answers give you insight into their thinking. It is not necessary for you to give an explanation.

7. Have each group of four children take their cups of ice to their dishpan of cool water. Have them put their cups in the water. (After the youngsters put the cups in the water, the ice should slide out of the cups.) Let the boys and girls play in the water with the ice.

8. Have the children remove the cups from the water before you begin Making a Home for Penguins.

The children learn from each other. In one class a preschool child asked, "Can we take the ice home?" His friend answered, "We can't take it home because it will melt."

Making a Home for Penguins

1. Say, "Some penguins live on the ice that's in water. Let's put our chunks of ice in the water."

2. Show the youngsters the ice in a milk carton. Allow time for them to comment on the shape of the ice. (As ice freezes, it expands. The expansion creates interesting bulges that often split open the sides of the milk carton.)

3. Ask, "What do you think will happen when I put this ice in the water?"

4. Gently place a chunk of ice in each pan of water. (If you can't remove the ice from the milk carton, put the milk carton in the water. As the ice melts, it will slide out of the carton. Then remove the carton.) The children may notice the ice melting and floating as they play with it.

Here Come the Penguins and Fish

This activity provides an opportunity for you to observe how much the children learn about floating, melting ice, and changing water temperature.

1. Give each child a cork and say, "Let's pretend the corks are penguins."

2. Ask, "Where could your penguin live?" [on the ice]

3. Let the children play with their penguins on the ice and in the water.

4. Put four plastic fish in each pan of water and ask, "What animals do you see in the water that penguins eat?" [fish]

5. Encourage the children to let their penguins slide on their bellies on the ice, "swim" in the water, and "eat" fish.

6. Gather the children in a circle on the floor. Encourage them to talk about what they did with the water, ice, penguins, and fish.

7. Ask, "Would you like to live in a home of ice and water?" "Why?" "What would you need?" "What would you do on ice?"

Role-Playing Penguins

1. Let the children pretend they are penguins and waddle and shuffle around on the "ice."

2. Encourage them to role play some of the other things penguins do, such as:
   - Swim.
   - Eat fish.

One teacher had her children wear paper penguin wings. She designated "ocean" and "ice" areas outside for role-playing penguins. If done in winter where there is snow, the children could role play outdoors.

Session 3: Making Comparisons

Some children are sensitive about their height. If this is the case in your class, mention the advantages of being tall or short before starting this activity.

What You Need

For the whole group
- ❏ 1 Emperor Penguin poster
- ❏ 1 roll of masking tape
- ❏ 1 marker

optional
- ❏ 1 full-length mirror
- ❏ 1–3 rolls of adding machine tape

For each child
- ❏ 1 sheet of paper about the size of the child
- ❏ An assortment of crayons

Getting Ready

Anytime Before the Activity

Optional

Hang the mirror on the wall so the children can see themselves next to the poster.

Several Days Before the Activity

Arrange for adult volunteers to help you with the body tracings if the children in your class are too young to help.

Who is Taller, You or the Penguin?

1. Attach the Emperor Penguin poster to the wall so the penguin's feet touch the floor.

2. Tell the group that the penguin on the poster is a very special penguin called an *emperor penguin*, and emperor penguins are the biggest kind of penguin.

3. Say, "Real emperor penguins are the same size as the penguin on the poster."

4. Let the children take turns estimating their height compared with the emperor penguin on the poster. The questions you ask depend on the age and height of the children in your class.

The following questions are suggested:
- With preschool children who are unfamiliar with the concept of taller or shorter, start out by asking, "Do you think you are taller than the penguin?"
- Ask kindergartners, "Do you think you are taller or shorter than the penguin?"
- With tall kindergartners and first graders ask, "Where do you think the top of the penguin's head will reach on your body?" [your chest? shoulders? chin? nose?]

5. Let each child stand next to the Emperor Penguin poster to compare their height.

Optional
1. If you have a full-length mirror, encourage the children to look in the mirror to see themselves standing next to the poster.

One teacher had her students take turns standing in front of a chalkboard next to the penguin poster and she marked their heights on the board.

More Comparisons

1. Have each child lie down on a sheet of paper that is about the same size as the child. Use a marker to draw around the child. Draw as carefully and as aesthetically as possible because some children may be offended if the drawing isn't "pretty."

2. Let the children color the drawings to make them look like themselves.

3. Hold one drawing at a time next to the penguin poster. Encourage each child to compare characteristics of the penguin drawing with his or her drawing. They can look at the heads, flippers, arms, legs, feet, and body. They can look for fingers, toes, and hair. They can also compare the colors in the two drawings.

Extensions for First Graders

1. After the children color their body tracing, encourage them to label their body parts on the tracing.

2. Use adding machine tape to measure your students. Cut strips the length of the children and let them hang the strips next to the penguin poster forming a bar graph.

If the children are sensitive about their height, tell them not to write their names on the strips.

Activity 2: The Emperor Penguin

Overview

After playing with the fish, ice, water, and cork penguins in Activity 1, the children know that penguins live in a cold home, swim, and eat fish. In this activity, they look at a life-size drawing of an emperor penguin and discover that penguins are birds with feathers, a beak, wings, and a tail. The girls and boys discover that feathers keep penguins warm just as clothing keeps people warm. The youngsters learn more about emperor penguins when they watch a drama about parent penguins caring for their eggs and young.

The boys and girls make paper-bag penguins and play with them on a large sheet of paper, which represents ice floating in an ocean. The children role-play penguins eating fish, snuggling together to stay warm, and holding eggs on their feet to keep the eggs off the cold ice. When paper baby penguins hatch from the eggs, the children create their own dramas of mother and father penguins taking care of their young.

Session 1: Getting to Know More About Penguins

What You Need

For the whole group
- ❏ 1 Emperor Penguin poster
- ❏ Several feathers (Buy the feathers at a craft store or have the children bring them from home.)
- ❏ 1 ice chest

For each child and yourself
- ❏ 1 glove, mitten, or large, thick sock
- ❏ 1 ice cube

Getting Ready

Put the ice cubes in the ice chest and bring it to class.

The Emperor Penguin Poster

1. Gather the children in a half circle on the floor in an area where the whole group can see the Emperor Penguin poster.

2. Ask questions to help the children remember what they learned about penguins, such as:
   - What are some of the things penguins do?
   - Where do you think emperor penguins live? [on the ice and in the water]

3. Have the youngsters take turns identifying the penguin body parts by pointing to the penguin's wings, feet, tail, eyes, and mouth. Ask, "What is another word for the penguin's mouth?" [beak]

4. Ask, "What do you think a penguin does with its beak?" [catches fish]

5. Ask, "What colors do you see on the emperor penguin?" [black, white, orange, or yellow]

Feathers

1. Have the children pass the feathers around so that each child has a chance to hold one.

2. Where do you think there are feathers on a penguin? [head, body, wings]

3. Have the children take turns pointing to the places on the emperor penguin where they think there are feathers.

Staying Warm

One teacher had each child hold a thick pile of feathers in one hand. The teacher put one ice cube on top of the feathers and another cube on the child's bare hand. The child felt immediately how feathers keep penguins warm.

1. Have each child put a mitten, glove, or sock on one hand.

2. Put an ice cube into each child's covered hand.

3. Tell the youngsters to count with you to five.

4. Have them hold the ice in the uncovered hand and count with you to five.

5. Ask, "Which hand stays warmer, the hand with the mitten or the hand without?" [the hand with the mitten]

6. Tell the children that mittens keep their hands warm from ice cubes just like feathers keep penguins warm from cold ice.

7. Ask questions that encourage the children to think about the clothes they wear to keep different parts of their bodies warm, such as:
   - What do you wear to keep your body warm? [coats, sweaters, jackets]
   - What do you wear to keep your legs warm? [pants, skirts, tights]
   - How do you keep your feet warm? Your head warm?

Session 2: Making Paper-Bag Penguins

Choices For Making Paper-Bag Penguins

Depending on your teaching approach and the skills of the children, you may choose to have the youngsters design their own paper penguins or follow the directions for making penguins that focus on penguin body structure.

The Child-Designed Penguin

If the children have the necessary skills, let them design, cut out, and assemble their own penguins. Some children may choose to make paper-bag penguins. Others may draw and cut out paper penguins. These penguins may be somewhat realistic or very imaginative. The purpose of this approach is to encourage the children's creativity and promote their independence.

The boys and girls need brown or white paper lunch bags, sheets of black and white construction paper, scissors, glue, and black, orange, and yellow crayons.

The Penguin Model

The process of assembling pre-cut penguin parts encourages the children to think about what a real penguin has on its body as they make a penguin with eyes, a beak, two wings, two feet, and a tail. Although structured, it allows for individual expression in the placement of the body parts. No two penguins ever look alike.

If you select this approach, you need to prepare materials in advance. Directions are in the three sections that follow.

What You Need

For the whole group

❏ 1 each of the following patterns: Pattern A (penguin beak),
   Pattern B (penguin wing), and Pattern C (penguin foot).
   (Master drawings are on page 27. A perforated copy for you
   to tear out is at the back of this guide on page 61.)
❏ 1 tray
❏ 1 large pair of scissors
❏ Enough newspaper to cover the work table(s) and tray

For each child and yourself

❏ 1 brown or white paper lunch bag
❏ 1 sheet of black paper (9" x 12")
❏ 1 black marker, or pencil
❏ 1 orange or yellow crayon
❏ 1 container of glue
optional

   ❏ 1 white crayon, or piece of white chalk, if you use brown
      bags and want to color the penguin's stomach

Getting Ready

Anytime Before the Activity

1. Cut two penguin beaks (Pattern A), two wings (Pattern B),
   and two feet (Pattern C) out of black paper for each paper-
   bag penguin. You need one penguin for each child and one
   for yourself.

2. Prepare the paper bags. (See the drawings on this and the
   next page.)
   • Cut the top of each paper bag to form a point that
     matches the shape of the penguin's beak.
   • Fold over the top third of the bag to make the head.

   Optional
   • You may want to glue the beaks on the bags ahead of
     time for very young children.

Immediately Before the Activity

1. Place one paper bag, two penguin beaks, two wings, two feet,
   one marker, one container of glue, and newspaper on a tray.
   Put the tray in the discussion area.

2. In the work area, spread newspapers on the tables and put one paper bag, two penguin beaks, two wings, two feet, one marker, and one container of glue at each child's place.

Making Paper-Bag Penguins

1. Tell the children they are going to make emperor penguins. Show them the paper bag and paper beak.

2. Ask, "Where do you think the penguin's beak belongs?" Have a child point to the top of the bag shaped like the beak.

3. Show the children how the shape of the penguin's beak matches the shape of the top of the bag. Glue on the two beak parts.

    The penguin's beak is an important orientation point for young children. Establish where the beak belongs before the children make their penguins.

4. Open and close the beak to show how the penguin uses its mouth.

5. Show the children where to write their names by writing your name on the backside of the paper-bag penguin.

6. Have the penguin face the group and ask, "What does this penguin need?" [eyes, wings, feet, tail]

7. Draw the eyes and tail. Glue on the wings and feet as the youngsters name the body parts.

8. Use the orange or yellow crayon to color the ear patches on the sides of the penguin's neck.

    Optional
        Use the white crayon, or chalk, to color the penguin's stomach.

9. Send the children to the work tables to make their penguins. Have each child glue the two beak pieces on the paper bag before adding the other penguin parts. Write the children's names for them if they can't write their own names.

10. Give the youngsters orange, yellow, or white crayons to color their penguins.

Having the children assist you in making the paper-bag penguin helps them visualize the finished penguin. Their comments, as they think through the process with you, provide an important review for the children and feedback for you.

Several teachers stuffed the paper-bag penguins with newspaper to make them stand up.

Session 3: Penguin Families

What You Need

For the whole group
- ❏ 1 Emperor Penguin poster
- ❏ Several Baby Emperor Penguin drawings on pages 29 and 67
- ❏ Several Emperor Penguin Egg drawings on pages 28 and 63
- ❏ 1 or more Baby Penguins Activity Sheets on pages 31 and 69
- ❏ 1 sheet of white paper, a white sheet, or a pillowcase (18" x 24", or larger)
- ❏ 1 sheet of blue paper, or a blue sheet, or rug (36" x 48", or larger)
- ❏ 1 sheet of yellow or orange paper (9" x 12")
- ❏ 1 large pair of scissors
- ❏ 1 Pattern D (fish) on pages 27 and 61

For each child and yourself
- ❏ 1 paper-bag penguin, or 1 child-designed penguin
- ❏ 1 pinch of cotton or pillow stuffing (you need an extra pinch for the drama)
- ❏ 1 container of white glue
- ❏ 1 hollow plastic egg large enough for a paper baby penguin to fit inside (you need an extra egg for the drama)

Many variety, grocery, and drug stores sell plastic eggs only before Easter. If eggs aren't available, ask parents to collect for you the plastic eggs that they may have around the house.

Getting Ready

Anytime Before the Activity

1. Cut one fish (Pattern D) out of yellow or orange paper for each child and for yourself, and several for the drama. Or have the children design and cut out their own fish.

2. Cut the large sheet of white paper into a jagged shape to resemble floating ice. (See the drawing on page 21.)

3. Copy the Baby Penguins Activity Sheet and cut out the baby penguins. You need one for each child, one for yourself, and one for the drama.

4. Make a baby penguin for the drama by gluing cotton or pillow stuffing onto one of the baby penguins you cut out. Put it in an egg and place the egg with the paper ice and water.

5. Put one baby penguin for each child and yourself inside a plastic egg and put the eggs aside to distribute later.

Playing with Penguins

1. Place the paper iceberg and blue paper water on the floor. Have the children place their paper-bag or self-designed penguins on the ice and in the water.

2. Allow time for the children to play with their penguins.

The Penguin Drama

1. Gather the children on the floor in a half circle around the paper water, ice, and penguins. Place several paper fish on the paper water.

2. Present a drama about parent penguins caring for their eggs and young. Use the props to act out penguin behaviors. Allow time for the children to express their own ideas when you ask them what the penguin can do.

- A mother penguin stands on the cold ice. She's about to lay an egg, but she doesn't have a soft nest to keep the egg warm. What can she do?
- She places her egg on her big feet. When the egg is on her feet, it doesn't touch the cold ice.
- She keeps the egg close to her warm body, and her fat, feathery belly hangs over the egg. The egg stays very warm.
- The mother penguin stands over her egg and keeps it warm.
- Soon she gets tired and very hungry.
- The father penguin waddles slowly over to the mother. He rolls the egg onto his feet and covers it with his warm, fat, feathery belly. Now it is his turn to take care of the egg.
- The hungry mother penguin waddles over the ice and dives into the water. She swims off to find fish to eat.
- The father penguin keeps the egg warm, but he begins to get very, very cold.
- He sees other father penguins who are keeping their eggs warm. An icy cold wind is blowing. Those fathers are also very cold.
- The fathers know what to do to stay warm. They snuggle close together in one big group. They keep each other warm for a long, long time.
- One day the egg begins to crack. What's happening? Very soon a fluffy white baby penguin comes out of the egg.
- The father penguin is tired and hungry, and has nothing to give the baby penguin to eat.
- Just then the mother penguin with a beak full of fish swims by. She climbs out of the water and onto the ice.
- The mother finds her baby penguin and gives it as much fish as it can eat.
- The tired, hungry father penguin waddles over the ice and dives into the water. He swims away to find fish to eat, and catches more fish to bring back to the baby penguin.

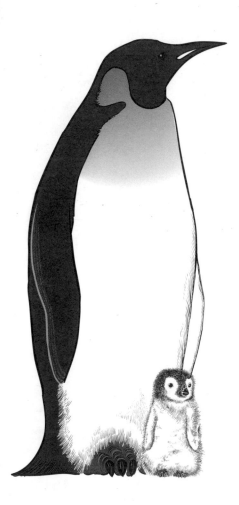

Role-Playing Parent Penguins

1. Pretend with the children that everyone is a penguin on the cold ice. Waddle and shuffle around like penguins.

2. Pretend that an icy cold wind is blowing, and all the penguins are getting very, very cold.

3. Ask, "What can the penguins do to stay warm?" [snuggle together] Gather all the youngsters close together so that everyone can feel the body warmth from the group.

4. Give each child a plastic egg with a paper baby penguin inside. Keep an egg for yourself.

5. Ask, "How can the penguins keep their eggs warm?" Have the youngsters stand and encourage them to try to hold the eggs on their feet.

6. Make cracking and peeping sounds and say, "I hear the eggs cracking open." Let the children open their eggs and play with their eggs and baby penguins. Notice if they hold the baby penguins on their feet.

Making Baby Penguins

1. Have the boys and girls bring their baby penguins and eggs to the circle. Have them find the baby penguin's eyes, beak, feet, and wings.

2. Open your egg and hold up the paper baby penguin so that all the children can see it. Glue cotton or pillow stuffing onto the baby penguin.

3. Have each child glue cotton or pillow stuffing onto his or her baby penguin.

Playing with Baby Penguins and Their Parents

1. Encourage the children to place their baby penguins on the paper ice with the parent penguins and create their own dramas.

2. When the youngsters are ready to take their penguins, eggs, and baby penguins home, give each child a paper fish. The children can perform penguin dramas at home for their families and friends.

One teacher gave the children fish-shaped crackers for the paper-bag penguins to "catch."

Comparisons

1. Show the Baby Emperor Penguin drawing to the group. Encourage the children to talk about what they see in the drawing. Have them find the baby penguin's eyes, beak, feet, and wings.

2. Place the drawing next to the drawing of the adult penguin. Ask, "How is the baby penguin different from the big penguin?" [It's smaller. It has more white on its face.]

3. Show the Emperor Penguin Egg drawing. Tell the children the egg is the same size as a real emperor penguin egg. Ask, "Do you think the egg is bigger or smaller than your foot?" "Your hand?"

4. Let the children take turns placing a hand and then a foot on the egg to find out which is bigger.

5. Let the children compare the length of the baby emperor penguin with their hands, feet, and anything they may find in the room.

Comparing Penguins with Other Birds

1. Ask, "What does a penguin have that other birds have?" [beaks, feathers, wings, feet, eyes, tail]

2. Ask, "What does a penguin do that other birds do?" [lays eggs]

3. Compare the Emperor Penguin poster with pictures of birds familiar to the children, or bring a live bird into class for the comparison.

Going Further

1. Encourage the children to paint or draw penguin pictures and make up penguin stories. They can write the stories or dictate them to you.

2. Have the children make up puppet dramas or plays to perform for the class.

3. If your school is in a snow area, encourage the children to think of penguin activities to do in the snow and on the ice.

Session 4 : A Penguin Parent

What You Need

For the whole group
- ❑ 1 black adult-size jacket or sweater
- ❑ 1 pillow in a white, preferably king-size, pillowcase
- ❑ 1 piece of white yarn, or a sash long enough to tie around a child's chest
- ❑ 1 plastic egg

optional
- ❑ 1 toy penguin

A Penguin Parent

1. Gather the children on the floor in a circle and ask, "How does a penguin mother or father keep its egg warm?" [puts the egg on its feet. Its warm feathery belly covers the egg.]

2. Ask for a volunteer to pretend to be a mother or father penguin.

3. Tie the top of the pillowcase around the child's chest so that the bottom of the pillow touches the child's feet.

4. Help the youngster put on the jacket.

5. Give the plastic egg to the child, and ask him to show the group how a penguin keeps its egg warm. (When he puts the egg on his feet, the bottom of the pillow covers the egg just as a penguin's warm feathery belly does.)

6. Leave the penguin costume out so other children can dress up like a penguin.

Optional
   Let the "penguin" hold a baby penguin (toy penguin) on her feet and under her flap to keep it warm.

Going Further

Encourage the children to try balancing objects on their feet. They can try blocks, sponges, small toys, and paper.

Extensions for First Graders

One teacher had her students draw penguins on peel-and-stick dots to place on the globe.

1. Encourage first graders to learn about different types of penguins by bringing penguin books to class to read. The children may be interested in the small size of the little blue penguin, the unusual appearance and fascinating behavior of the rockhopper penguin, and the nesting behavior of the Adélie penguin. See "Resources" on pages 53 and "Background Information" on pages 47.

2. Give your students an idea of where penguins live by showing them a globe. (Use a globe instead of a map because first graders have difficulty conceptualizing the world as a ball.) To familiarize them with the globe, ask for volunteers to point to the water and land areas. Point out where the children live. Let the youngsters place stickers, preferably penguin stickers, in the areas where penguins live. Penguins are found along the coasts of Antarctica, southern Australia, in the south and on the west coast of South America, South Africa, New Zealand, and the Galápagos Islands. (See the map on page 46.)

3. Provide opportunities for the children to compare the animal life in the Arctic and Antarctic regions. See "Resources" on page 53 and "Background Information" on page 47.

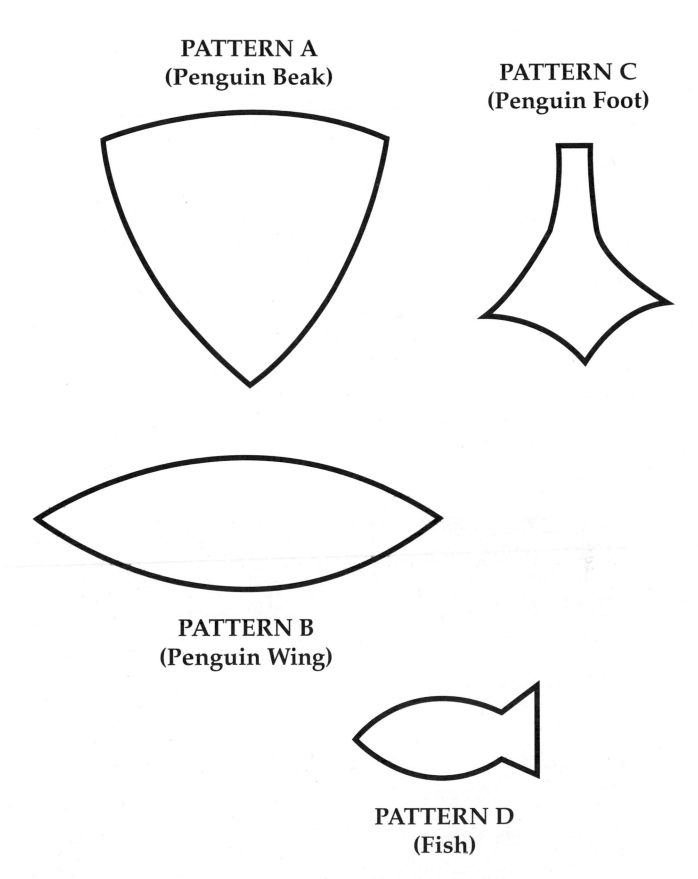

PATTERN A
(Penguin Beak)

PATTERN C
(Penguin Foot)

PATTERN B
(Penguin Wing)

PATTERN D
(Fish)

Cut two of each pattern (except the fish) when making a Paper-Bag Penguin.

Paper-Bag Penguin Patterns

Emperor Penguin Egg

Baby Emperor Penguin

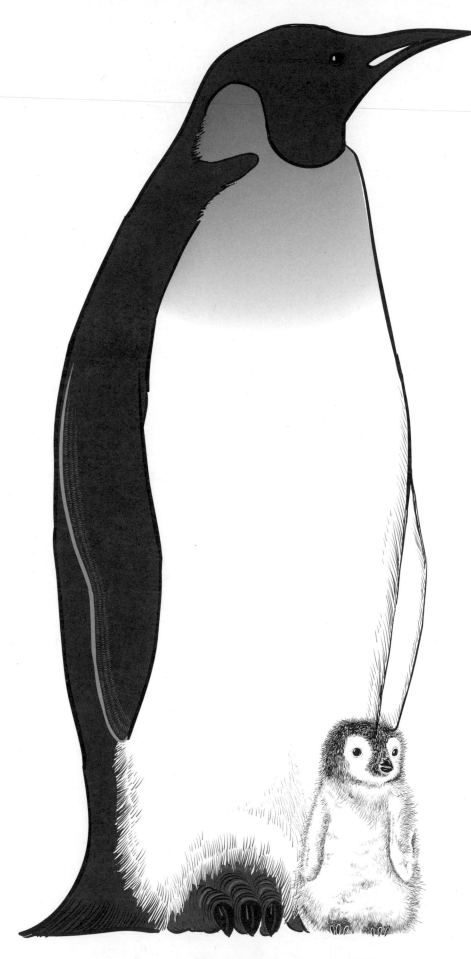

Emperor Penguin and Baby

Baby Penguins Activity Sheet

31

Activity 3: Hungry Young Penguins

Overview

The children pretend they are hungry young penguins and "catch" fish (fish crackers) to eat. They continue in their roles as penguins and play the Hungry Penguins Game. This game gives children practice with number concepts including counting, one-to-one correspondence, addition, and subtraction. The children use concrete materials—fish crackers and paper oceans—to understand the operations of addition and subtraction. The game also develops problem-solving and story-problem skills. The Hungry Penguins Game can be adapted to your children's abilities by adjusting the number of fish you use.

Session 1: Penguins Eating Fish

What You Need

For the whole group
- ❏ 1 sheet of blue paper (12" x 18")
- ❏ 1 tray
- ❏ 1 bag of fish-shaped crackers

Getting Ready
Immediately Before the Activity

1. Cover the tray with the sheet of blue paper.

2. Place the fish crackers on the paper.

3. Have the children wash their hands to get ready for their penguin snack of fish crackers.

Macaroni Penguin

Role-Playing Hungry Young Penguins

One teacher gave her class a snack of real penguin food (sardines, shrimp, and squid) for the penguin snack.

1. Gather the children in a group. Tell them that when baby penguins get bigger they stay together in a group. When they get much bigger, they swim in the water to find fish to eat.

2. Tell the youngsters that everyone in the group is a hungry young penguin that is old enough to catch fish to eat.

3. Place the tray of fish on the table. Let the children take turns "catching" fish and eating them.

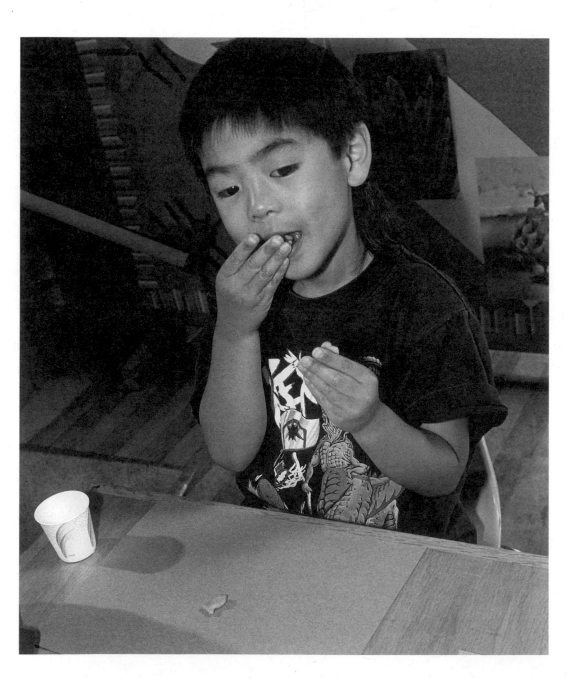

Session 2: Hungry Penguins Game

What You Need

For the whole group
❑ 2 bags of fish-shaped crackers

For each child and yourself
❑ 1 sheet of blue paper (8½" x 11")
❑ 1 paper cup (5 oz.)

Getting Ready

1. Fill a cup with fish crackers for each child and yourself.

Hungry Penguins Catch Fish

1. Give each child a sheet of blue paper. Have the children pretend that the blue paper is an ocean. Ask what lives in the ocean. Ask what penguins eat. [fish, squid, krill—small shrimp-like creatures]

2. Distribute the cups of fish crackers. Ask the children to pretend they are hungry penguins and that their crackers are fish.

3. Tell the children a story similar to the one that follows. As you tell the story, invite the children to follow along and be the hungry penguins.

   • One day there were two fish swimming in the ocean. (Put two crackers on the blue paper ocean to represent the two fish in the ocean. Have the children each place two fish crackers on their oceans.)

   • As the fish were swimming, two more fish joined them. (Add two more crackers to the ocean.) Ask, "How many fish are there in the ocean now?" [four]

   • As the fish were swimming, a hungry penguin dove into the water and ate one of the fish. (Model being a hungry penguin and eat one of the fish crackers. Have the children do the same.) Ask, "How many fish are left?" [three]

   • Two more fish joined the three fish that were left. (Add two more fish crackers.) Ask, "How many fish are there in the ocean?" [five]

- A very hungry penguin dove into the ocean and ate four fish. (Have all the children eat four fish from their ocean.) Ask, "How many fish are left?" [one]

- That one little fish joined three other fish. Ask, "How many fish are in the ocean?" [four]

- A hungry penguin dove into the ocean to eat some fish. The fish all got away! Ask, "How many fish are left?" [four]

4. The story continues with everyone adding and taking away—by eating—the fish. As you model the story, try to have the hungry penguin eat various numbers of fish, but not all of them. You can increase or decrease the numbers of fish depending on the abilities of your children. After the children are familiar with the way the game is played, they can take turns continuing the story, which helps develop their language and mathematical skills.

Hungry Penguins Game with Toy Fish

Children can play this game independently after it has been modeled. You may want to have plastic or rubber fish available instead of the fish crackers. Children can tell each other the story and place fish on and off the blue paper ocean as the story is told. Older children can record the fish story with equations.

In another version of this game, have two children start with a small number of fish in the ocean. One child closes her eyes while the other child takes some fish away. The first child opens her eyes and guesses how many were taken away. Be sure students keep the number of fish they start with appropriate to their abilities.

Extensions for Kindergartners and First Graders

Recording the Story with Numbers

As you tell the story, you can record the data of the number of fish being eaten by the penguins as equations. However, we suggest you play the game at least once without equations so the children are familiar with it.

After two fish are put in the ocean, write the number 2 on the board to represent those two fish. When two more fish are added to the ocean, write a plus 2 (+ 2) on the board to represent those you are adding. Ask, "How many fish are there in the ocean now?" Make an equals sign (=) and write the total number of fish (four) to complete that equation (2 + 2 = 4).

Have the students look at their oceans again. How many fish are there? Rewrite the number 4 to start a new equation. Next, take away one fish (have the children eat one fish). Record taking away one fish, write minus 1 (– 1) on the board. Ask the children how many fish are left. Finish the equation by writing an equals sign and record the answer (4 – 1 = 3).

After each equation is completed be sure to rewrite the answer, as it will be the first part of the next equation. That number is also the number of fish that should be on each child's ocean.

After you have modeled the recording process at least one time without the children recording, you may want to have older children record the equations simultaneously to keep track of the eaten fish. This will tell the story in numbers.

Activity 4: More Fun with Ice

Overview

The children learn how ice can have many shapes, colors, and flavors in this series of short, ice activities. They create colored ice shaped like hands, balloons, or shells. The children use their prior information to set up simple ice investigations and, best of all, they prepare and eat delicious ice treats with frozen fruit inside.

This series of activities is a wonderful culmination to the previous ice explorations. Giving the children this rich experience is well worth the extra effort.

Session 1: Making Ice Shapes

What You Need

For the whole group

- ❏ Several sturdy, waterproof trays
- ❏ An assortment of interesting objects that hold water, such as balloons, large half shells (scallop, clam, or abalone), plastic cups, plastic bags, plastic sand molds, and rubber gloves. (Each child chooses one object. Have extra balloons in case each child chooses a balloon.)
- ❏ 1 twist-tie for each balloon and rubber glove

optional

  - ❏ 3 bottles of food coloring—one bottle of each of the following colors: red, blue, and yellow

For each group of four children

- ❏ 1 large dishpan about 20" x 15" x 5"
- ❏ 1 towel

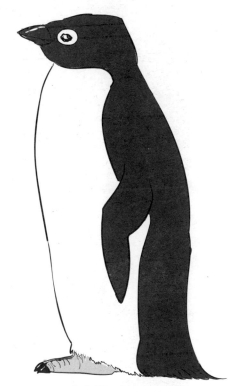

Adélie Penguin

Getting Ready

Several Days Before the Activity

1. Arrange for adult help to supervise small groups of children.

2. Encourage the children to bring in small containers that hold water, such as plastic sand molds, or they can look around the classroom for items that can hold water.

Immediately Before the Activity

1. Fill one dishpan with water for each group of four children.

2. Place at least four objects in each pan.

Optional

   Food coloring in the water produces interesting effects when the water freezes. Use it to make the water in each pan a different color. Use the coloring sparingly because too much color stains the children's skin and clothes.

Making Shapes

1. Let four children at a time gather around each pan of water and play with the objects in the water.

2. As they begin to lose interest in the water ask, "What do you think will happen if we fill the balloons, shells, gloves, and cups with water, then put them in the freezer?" Allow time for the children to express their own ideas.

3. Let each child choose one object to fill with water.

4. Help the children fill the balloons with water by attaching the end of each balloon to a faucet. Fill until the balloon is about the size of a lemon.
   Filling balloons with water can be problematic, but it is worth the extra effort because of the interesting ice shapes produced. Carefully supervise a few children at a time as they fill the balloons, or fill them yourself.

5. Use the twist-ties to tightly close the balloons and gloves.

6. Have each child place the object he or she chose on the tray.

7. If possible, let the children watch as you place the objects in the freezer.

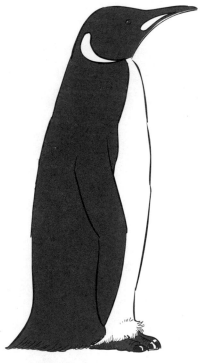

King Penguin

Session 2: Ice Shapes

What You Need

For the whole group

❏ Several sturdy, waterproof trays
❏ An assortment of frozen objects, still in their containers, from Session 1
❏ 1 large dishpan about 20" x 15" x 5"
❏ 1 towel
optional
  ❏ 1 ice chest

Ice chests are an efficient way to transport the ice and keep it frozen during the class session.

Getting Ready

Several Days Before the Activity

Arrange for adult help to supervise small groups of children.

Immediately Before the Activity

Fill the dishpan with cool water.

Discovering Strange and Beautiful Shapes

1. When the water in the objects is frozen, take the children in small groups to remove the objects from the freezer, or ice chest.

2. Encourage the children to gently touch the objects and the ice.

3. Use the trays to carry the ice to the tables. Ask, "How can we get the ice out of the balloons without breaking the balloons?"

4. Let the boys and girls try the ideas they suggest. They may say, "Let the ice melt" or "Put the balloons in water" or "Hold the balloons."

5. Let them try out their ideas with the other frozen shapes.

6. Let the ice in the glove melt enough so that you can gently slide the glove off without breaking the fingers of ice.

7. Give the children time to freely explore the ice objects in and out of water.

8. Observe if the children notice the following:
   • The shapes change as they melt.
   • Air bubble patterns, cracks, and (if you used food colors) color clumps in the ice.

9. If you made colored ice, listen to the children's comments as they observe the colored water from the ice mixing and creating new colors.

Going Further

1. After the children observe the ice shapes, let them make ice sculptures with the leftover ice by stacking one piece on top of another in the trays. Encourage the youngsters to check back later to see how their ice sculptures have changed.

2. If you celebrate Halloween with your class, prepare a spooky treat. Fill a rubber glove with water and put it in the freezer. Remove the frozen hand from the glove and place it in a punch bowl filled with bright red juice. Let the children drink the juice.

Session 3: Ice Investigations

In these investigations, it is not necessary for you or the children to come up with the "right" answer. Encourage the children to follow the process of guessing, observing, and suggesting possible reasons for what they see happening.

What You Need

For the whole group
❏ 2 large bowls
❏ 1 ice chest

For each child and yourself
❏ 2 small plastic cups (3–8 oz.)
❏ 6 or more ice cubes from an ice tray (ice cubes should be about the same size)

Getting Ready

Put the ice cubes in the ice chest and bring it to class.

Sun and Shade Investigation

When the children do their investigations, be sure to point out places where it is not safe to put ice, such as on electrical appliances.

1. Give each child a cup with two ice cubes the same size.

2. Ask, "What do you think will happen if you put one ice cube in the sun and one in the shade?" Ask, "Which one do you think will turn into water first?"

3. Encourage the children to experiment. Ask, "Which ice cube melted first?" [the one in the sun] Ask, "Why do you think the ice in the sun melted first?"

   It is important for the children to wonder why, but it is not necessary for you to tell them why.

Water and Ice Investigation

1. Fill one bowl with cold water and one bowl with warm water and put the bowls where the children can reach them.

2. Let the youngsters use their fingers to feel the temperature of the water in both bowls.

   The best way to introduce the concept of temperature to young children is for them to experience warmth and cold. In this activity, the children use their fingers to feel and compare the temperature of warm and cold water. They do not need thermometers to conduct this investigation.

3. Give each child a cup with two ice cubes the same size.

4. Ask, "If you put one ice cube in cold water and one ice cube in warm water, which one do you think will melt first?"

5. Have the children try it and find out. Then ask:
   • What did you do?
   • What happened?
   • Why do you think the ice in the warm water melted first?
   • Were you surprised? Why?

More Melting Investigations

1. Encourage the children to come up with their own investigations. They can work individually or in small groups.

2. After each child or group has completed the investigation, re-ask the questions in #5 above to encourage the children to think about the process of setting up an investigation, making predictions, observing, and discussing the results.

Session 4: Making Ice Treats

What You Need

For the whole group
- ❏ Enough fruit juice for each child to have two 3 oz. cups
- ❏ 1 waterproof marking pen
- ❏ 1 freezer
- ❏ 1 tray

For each child and yourself
- ❏ 1 paper cup (3 oz.)
- ❏ Several berries, slices of banana, and/or orange or apple sections with no seeds

Getting Ready

Anytime Before the Activity

Use the waterproof pen to write a child's name on each cup.

Freezing Juice and Fruit

1. At snack time, give each child one half cup of fruit juice in his or her cup (remember the children's names are on the cups) and several pieces of fruit to drop into the juice. Have the boys and girls observe whether the fruit floats or sinks.

2. Let the children drink the juice and eat the fruit.

3. Ask, "What do you think will happen if we put cups of juice and fruit in the freezer?"

4. Again pour one half cup of juice in each cup, and let each youngster drop a piece of fruit into his or her cup.

5. Have the children put their cups on the tray and, if possible, let the youngsters watch as you put the cups in the freezer.

Session 5: Ice Treats

What You Need
For the whole group
❏ 1 freezer, or ice chest

For each child and yourself
❏ 1 cup of frozen juice and fruit from Session 4

Getting Ready
If the freezer is far from your classroom, put the frozen juice in an ice chest and bring it to class.

Frozen Juice and Fruit
1. When the juice is frozen, take the children with you to the freezer, or ice chest.

2. Give each child his or her cup. Ask, "What happened to the juice and fruit?" "Where is the fruit?"

3. Let the children examine their cups and take turns telling the group what happened.

4. Let the children eat the frozen juice and fruit.

Going Further
1. Put chunks of frozen juice and fruit in a bowl of fruit punch.

2. Encourage the children to watch the chunks melt and the pieces of fruit fall out of the frozen juice.

3. Let the children drink the punch and eat the fruit.

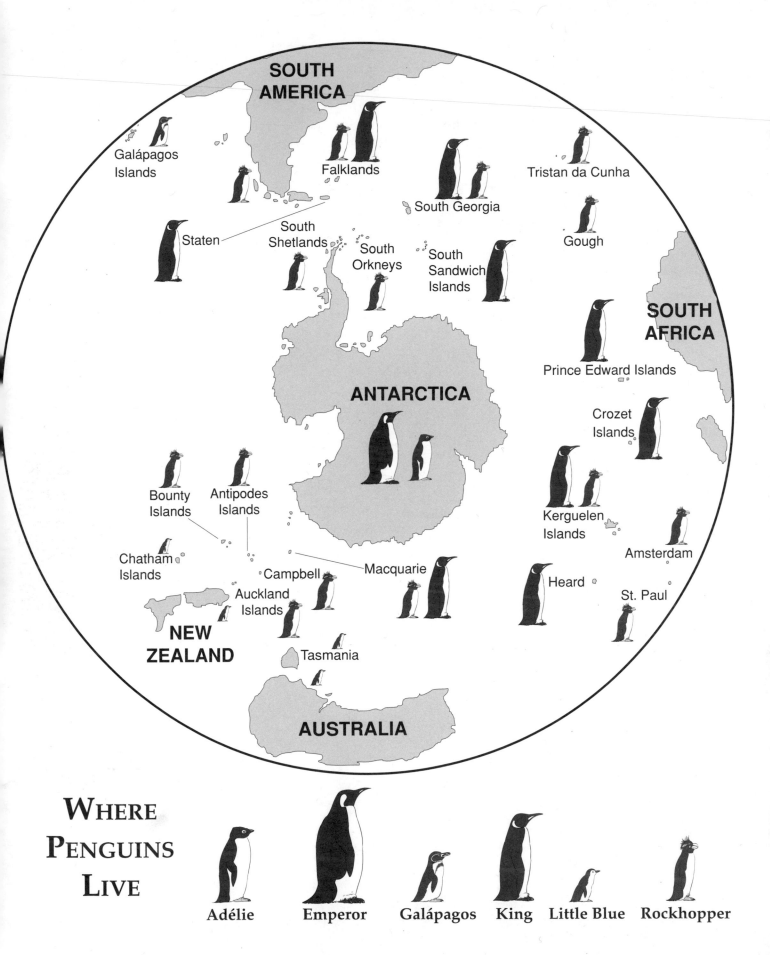

SOUTH
AMERICA

Galápagos
Islands

Falklands

Tristan da Cunha

South Georgia

Gough

Staten

South
Shetlands

South
Orkneys

South
Sandwich
Islands

SOUTH
AFRICA

Prince Edward Islands

ANTARCTICA

Crozet
Islands

Bounty
Islands

Antipodes
Islands

Kerguelen
Islands

Amsterdam

Chatham
Islands

Campbell

Macquarie

Heard

St. Paul

Auckland
Islands

NEW
ZEALAND

Tasmania

AUSTRALIA

WHERE
PENGUINS
LIVE

Adélie **Emperor** **Galápagos** **King** **Little Blue** **Rockhopper**

Background Information

A Variety of Penguins

The Southern Hemisphere is home to 18 species of penguins. Penguins live along the coast of Antarctica, in the south and on the west coast of South America, South Africa, Southern Australia, New Zealand, and the Galápagos Islands. Their habitats range from the barren ice of Antarctica, where Adélie and emperor penguins are found, to the tropical island home of the Galápagos penguins. No penguins live in the wild in the Northern Hemisphere.

Size, as well as habitat, varies greatly among penguins. The smallest penguin, the little blue or fairy penguin of Australia and New Zealand, is 16" tall and weighs less than 2½ lbs. The largest penguin, the emperor, may grow to almost 4' tall and weigh 100 lbs. Female penguins are slightly smaller than males.

Penguin behavior also varies among the different species. At nesting time, some penguins find shelter in underground caves, some dig burrows, while most species make nests of pebbles and grass. The emperor and king penguins make no nests at all. Since emperor penguins have no nests to defend, they are not territorial. They huddle peacefully together to stay warm. In all species, both male and female penguins take care of the young.

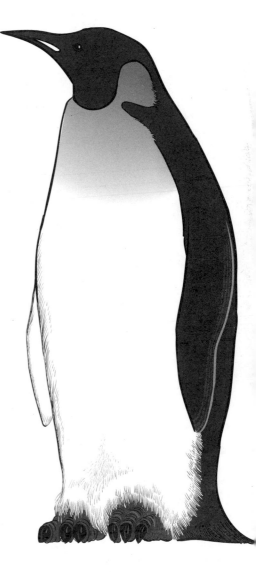

The Emperor Penguin
Courting and Parenting

During the early months of the Antarctic winter (late spring and early summer in the Northern Hemisphere), male and female emperor penguins court. To attract a mate, both females and males swing their heads from side to side to display the yellow and orange patches on the sides of their heads. Then, with heads against their chests, they trumpet loudly and melodiously.

Two months after mating, each female lays one cream-colored egg, which she holds on her feet and covers with a flap of belly skin and feathers. Shortly after laying, the females turn the job of incubating the eggs over to the males. The female emperors then leave to feed in the sea.

The father penguins keep the eggs warm for two months of near continuous darkness when temperatures may drop to -110° F. It is not uncommon for winds up to 180 mph to roar across the ice. Often thousands of males crowd together. Each penguin takes his turn standing in the center of the huddle, the warmest spot. When a male moves from one place to another, he shuffles with the egg on his large feet. He carefully keeps the egg

off the ice and close to his warm body, under his fold of belly skin and feathers.

Two months after the eggs are laid, they begin to hatch. At this time, each female penguin returns from the sea with her crop (a special stomach used to hold food) full of fish and squid to feed her young. The males, who have lost about 40 percent of their body weight, now go to sea to feed.

Baby Emperor Penguins

Newly hatched emperor penguins are grey with white faces surrounded by black down. When the young emperors are between six and nine weeks old, they leave the adults and huddle together in large groups. The adults continue to feed them, but the young are vulnerable to predators. (Two types of birds, kelp gulls and skuas, are constantly on the alert for penguin eggs and chicks to eat.)

When the young emperors are about six months old they molt. They resemble their parents, but are less colorful. The young penguins are now old enough to go to sea to feed. When they molt a second time, 18 months later, the young are indistinguishable from their parents. They are not mature enough to breed until they reach at least six years of age.

Locomotion

Emperor penguins are flightless birds. They use their wings as flippers to swim quickly and gracefully through the ocean waters. They are excellent swimmers and dive deeper in the water than any other bird. Emperor penguins can dive to almost 900 feet deep and stay submerged up to 20 minutes. When they walk, they waddle with their beaks held high. When the ice slopes, they lie flat on their bellies and slide along as if they were tobogganing.

Food

Penguins hunt in the sea for fish, squid, and krill (tiny shrimp-like creatures) to eat and feed to their young. They use their spiky beaks to hold these slippery ocean animals.

Enemies

In the ocean, orcas (killer whales) and leopard seals prey on emperor penguins. The leopard seal swims in a circle around a penguin until the penguin is exhausted. The seal then attacks the penguin and eats it. On land, adult emperor penguins have no enemies.

Defense

Penguins use their very strong beaks and their powerful club-like flippers to protect themselves and their young.

Life Span

Emperor penguins live over 30 years in captivity. It is unknown how long they live in the wild.

Other Species of Penguins

Including the emperor, there are 18 species of penguins: Adélie, Blackfooted, Chinstrap, Erect-Crested, Fiordland-Crested, Galápagos, Gentoo, King, Little Blue, Macaroni, Magellanic, Peruvian, Rockhopper, Royal, Snares-Crested, White-Flippered, and Yellow-Eyed.

The six penguins described in detail below were chosen because their size, appearance, habitat, and behavior, especially nesting behavior, make interesting comparisons with those of the emperor penguin. Unlike the emperor, these six penguins incubate their eggs during the summer months when there is no snow.

Adélie Penguin

The Adélie penguin (the most abundant of the penguins) lives on the Antarctic mainland, the Antarctic Peninsula, and on neighboring islands. Its distinguishing marks include a solid black head with a white circle around its eye and pink feet. These 30" tall penguins are often seen moving in a straight line across the ice, either walking or tobogganing.

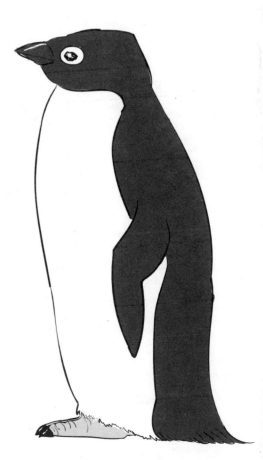

Adélies nest close together in the thousands, usually on a rocky headland. When the snow melts in the late spring or early summer, nesting begins. Each pair has their own small territory, which they defend aggressively. The male collects pebbles, sometimes stealing them from an unguarded nest, and takes them to the female, who stands on the nest site. He drops the pebbles at her feet and she builds a ring of pebbles around herself. She lays two greenish-white eggs, each two inches long, in the nest. Both parents take turns incubating the eggs and taking care of the young. At about one month old, the chicks form crèches. The parents still feed their young, and when a parent returns from the sea with food, it identifies its young by sound. The young recognizes its parent's voice and responds.

Little Blue Penguin

The little blue penguin, sometimes called the fairy penguin, is the smallest of all penguin species standing at about 16" tall. This bluish penguin with yellow eyes is found in New Zealand and Southern Australia. It is a more agile swimmer than larger penguins and spends much of its time floating on the surface of the water. Because of its small size, it is vulnerable to predatory birds, such as gulls, skuas, harriers, and eagles, and usually comes ashore after dark to hide in burrows where it nests.

Rockhopper Penguin

With a red beak, red eyes, yellow eyebrows and long yellow tufts of feathers on each side of its black head, the appearance of the rockhopper is striking. This two-foot-tall penguin lives on the Falkland Islands off the coast of Argentina, on South Georgia Island, and on several other islands in the southern Atlantic Ocean.

The rockhopper gets its name because it hops from rock to rock. It sometimes jumps six feet in a single hop. It often hops into the water feet first and leaves the sea by leaping up as much as four feet to a rocky ledge. On flat surfaces, some hop while others walk.

This cackling penguin, the noisiest of all penguins, nests high above the sea, often near the edge of cliffs. It makes a bowl of grass for a nest, or lays its two eggs directly on the rock. Both parents take turns incubating the eggs and caring for the chicks. When the chicks are about two weeks old, they join crèches, or nurseries, which provide protection from predators. A few adult penguins guard each crèche. At nine weeks, the young are full grown and go off to sea to feed.

Macaroni Penguin

Macaroni penguins are widespread on the Antarctic Peninsula and on islands in the southern Atlantic and Indian oceans. This colorful penguin with its red beak, red eyes, and long yellow head feathers gets its name from the fashionable dandies or "macaronies" of 18th century England. The macaronies wore feathers in their hats as satirized in the song "Yankee Doodle Dandy."

The macaroni penguin is similar to the rockhopper in appearance and behavior. They both have the same type nesting sites, sometimes nesting next to each other. It differs from the rockhopper in having a heavier bill, pink corners of the mouth, and its long yellow feathers form a crest over the forehead. Also, macaronies are a few inches taller than rockhoppers and have a nasal rat-a-tat-tat call.

King Penguin

The king penguin lives on the Falkland Islands, South Georgia, and several other islands surrounding the Antarctic continent. This three-foot-tall penguin resembles the emperor penguin, but is shorter, more slender, and its yellowish-orange ear patches form a comma shape on each side of its head.

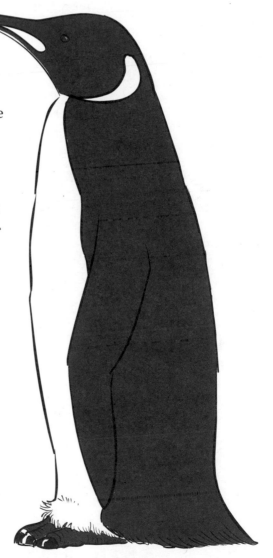

Unlike the emperor, each female king lays an egg during the Antarctic spring or summer and she shares the job of incubating the egg with the male. Like the emperor, king parents incubate their one egg by putting it on their feet and covering the egg with their belly flap. When the young are old enough, they join a crèche, and both parents bring food from the sea to the chick.

While the emperor penguins trumpet melodiously to attract mates, king penguins bray like donkeys.

King penguins have an interesting defense against leopard seals, predators of swimming penguins. When a king sees a seal, it panics and swims rapidly to shore beating its flippers on the surface of the water. The noise alerts other king penguins, who also rush to shore.

Galápagos Penguin

The Galápagos penguin is the next smallest penguin after the little blue. It breeds on the western shores of the Galápagos Islands (off the coast of Ecuador) where the water is the coldest. It nests in small groups or scattered pairs in caves formed by lava flows. This little penguin has two black stripes on its chest and a loud braying call. Like the little blue penguin, it usually comes ashore at night to sleep.

Penguin Conservation

Unfortunately, people are harming penguins by polluting the oceans, taking large supplies of fish, squid, and krill that penguins need for food, and by invading penguin nesting sites. The most endangered penguin is the Humboldt penguin. It nests on islands off the coasts of Chile and Peru, which are rich in guano (the manure of sea birds). Mining operations in the guano deposits, which are harvested for fertilizer, are destroying the burrows where the penguins nest. Also, the large number of anchovies caught each year for commercial purposes is drastically reducing the Humboldt penguin's food supply.

If penguins are to survive, people need to be more concerned about the amount of chemicals dumped and oil spilled in the ocean, and the amount of fish and seafood taken from the ocean. We also need to find ways to protect the nesting sites of these fascinating animals.

Animals of the Polar Regions

Adélie and emperor penguins, skuas, petrels, gulls, and terns are the few inhabitants of the ice-covered Antarctic continent. In the waters surrounding Antarctica, leopard seals swim, waiting for a penguin to eat. Weddell and elephant seals and several species of whales also feed in these southern waters.

By contrast, the Arctic abounds in a rich variety of animal life. The arctic hare, lemming, ptarmigan, reindeer, and musk ox flourish on the abundance of plant life during the brief Arctic summer. Snowy owls, weasels, foxes, and wolves hunt the plant-eating animals and thrive. Colonies of walruses sprawl on the rocky beaches and, out on the ice in winter, polar bears hunt for seals. In the icy waters, various types of whales swim.

The polar regions are our last great wilderness areas. Learning about them helps children, our next generation, understand the importance of preserving the animals that live there.

Resources

Reference Books for Children

Arnold, Caroline. *Penguin.* New York: Morrow Junior Books, 1988.

Barrett, Norman. *Picture Library: Penguins.* New York: Franklin Watts, 1991.

Bonners, Susan. *A Penguin Year.* New York: Dell Publishing, 1981.

The Cousteau Society: Penguins. New York: Simon & Schuster, 1992.

Cowcher, Helen. *Antarctica.* New York: Scholastic, 1990.

Crow, Sandra Lee. *Penguins and Polar Bears.* Washington, D.C.: National Geographic Society, 1985.

Dalmais, Anne-Marie. *Animal World: The Penguin.* Mahwah, N.J.: Watermill Press, 1983.

Fontanel, Beatrice. *Animal Close-ups: The Penguin.* Watertown, MA: Charlesbridge Publishing, 1992.

Kalman, Bobbie. *Arctic Animals.* Toronto: Crabtree Publishing, 1988.

Lepthien, Emilie V. *A New True Book: Penguins.* Chicago: Children's Press, 1983.

Ling, Mary. *See How They Grow: Penguin.* London: Dorling Kindersley, 1993.

Paladino, Catherine. *Pomona: The Birth of a Penguin.* New York: Franklin Watts, 1991.

Robertson, Graham. "Project Penguin," *Ranger Rick* (December 1991): pages 3–9.

Robinson, Claire. *Life Story: Penguin.* Mahwah, N.J.: Troll Associates, 1994.

Royston, Angela. *The Penguin.* Nashville: Ideals Publishing, 1988.

Serventy, Vincent. *Animals in the Wild: Penguin.* New York: Scholastic, 1983.

Wexo, John Bonnett. *Zoobooks: Penguins.* San Diego: Wildlife Education, 1988.

Video

Penguin Odyssey. San Francisco: Marine Mammal Fund, 1988.

Internet: World Wide Web

The Penguin Page. http://www.vni.net/~kwelch/penguins

Reference Books for Adults

Burton, Dr. Maurice and Burton, Robert. "Emperor penguin," *The International Wildlife Encyclopedia*: 720–724. New York: Marshall Cavendish, 1969.

Gorman, James. *The Total Penguin.* New York: Prentice Hall, 1990.

Kaehler, Wolfgang. *Penguins.* San Francisco: Chronicle Books, 1989.

Peterson, Roger Tory. *Penguins.* Boston: Houghton Mifflin, 1979.

54

Literature Connections

Antarctica
by Helen Cowcher
Scholastic, New York. 1990
Grades: Preschool–1

Although this is a nonfiction book, it is an exciting and dramatic tale about emperor penguins and contemporary life in Antarctica. The story neatly dovetails with all the ideas in the drama in Activity 2 and extends them by introducing other animals that live on and around the icy continent. The impact people have on the animals and the habitat of Antarctica is also presented. The text and large, colorful illustrations provide a resource for first graders who compare the Arctic and Antarctic regions as well as the nesting behaviors of the Adélie and emperor penguins.

Little Penguin
by Patrick Benson
Philomel Books, New York. 1990
Grades: Preschool–1

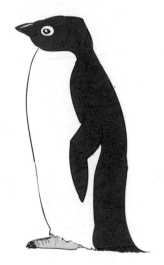

Little Penguin is the story of Pip, an Adélie penguin who wants to be as big as an emperor penguin. As Pip playfully explores the snow, ice, and water of her Antarctic home, she wonders why some animals are big and some small. This story ties in beautifully with the activities on relative sizes in *Penguins And Their Young*. The children can use the illustrations to compare the appearance of Adélie penguins with emperor penguins.

Mr. Popper's Penguins
by Richard and Florence Atwater
Little, Brown & Co., Boston. 1938
Grades: K–6

This well-loved classic about Mr. Popper's experiences with a house full of curious Adélie penguins delights children. Relevant chapters include Chapter IV: Captain Cook, in which the penguin Captain Cook eats Mr. Popper's goldfish, and Chapter VII: Captain Cook Builds A Nest, in which the penguin collects marbles, a half-eaten lollipop, and other miscellaneous objects resembling stones, to build a nest in the refrigerator. At one point Mr. Popper dresses up like a penguin and shuffles around the house.

My Friend the Penguin
by Jeffrey Schneider
Educational Products, San Francisco. 1991
Grades: Preschool–K

This board book has fun illustrations and a delightful poem about penguins. It makes a wonderful read-aloud book for younger children.

**Out on the Ice
in the Middle of the Bay**
by Peter Cumming
Annick Press, Toronto. 1993
Grades: Preschool–2

The little Eskimo girl Leah wanders away from home and encounters a baby polar bear whose mother is close by. Leah's father plans to shoot the mother bear to save his child and the mother bear prepares to destroy the man to defend her cub. This suspenseful story gives children a view of Eskimo life in a contemporary Arctic setting, and the beautiful ending provides an alternative to violence in people's encroachment on nature. Although this book does not deal with penguins, first graders who compare the Arctic and Antarctic regions, in the Extensions for First Graders at the end of Activity 2, should find this story especially relevant.

Penguin Small
by Mick Inkpen
Harcourt, Brace, Jovanovich, San Diego. 1992
Grades: Preschool–1

This beautifully illustrated story about a penguin's journey from the North Pole to the South Pole provides many opportunities for young children to contrast some of the things the fictional Penguin Small does to what real penguins do. Read the story to the children after they learn about real penguin behaviors and habitats in Activity 1 and Activity 2. Since Penguin Small's behavior and encounters are so fantastic, children enjoy the comparison.

Pinkie Leaves Home
by Peter O'Donnell
Scholastic, New York. 1991
Grades: Preschool–1

Pinkie the Penguin, who lost all his feathers in an oil slick, does not like cold weather. One day he sets off to find a warm place by the sea where there is no ice and snow. This adventure story reinforces the concepts that feathers keep penguins warm, penguins eat fish, and penguins live by the sea. The story's surprise ending supports the idea that wearing a hat, scarf, and coat is a way of staying warm. This book provides an amusing extension to Activity 2, where the children learn about penguin feathers.

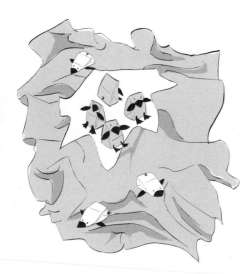

Summary Outlines

Activity 1: A Home of Ice and Water

Session 1: From Water to Ice
Water
> Let children play with cups, then milk cartons, in water.

Water Into Ice
> 1. Fill a milk carton with water and ask, "What do you think will happen to the water if we put it in the freezer?"
> 2. Let each child fill a cup with water.
> 3. Put cups and cartons in freezer.
> 4. With children, check water several times throughout the day.

Session 2: An Ice Home
Getting to Know Penguins
> 1. Ask children what animals live on ice. Ask, "What animal is black and white and lives on ice?"
> 2. Show Emperor Penguin poster and ask what animal it is.
> 3. Ask questions about penguins.
> 4. Ask a child to point out the penguin's wings. Tell the children penguins don't fly. Discuss the use of wings for swimming.
> 5. Ask and describe how penguins move on ice.

Ice and Water
> 1. Let children remove cups from freezer. Ask what happened to the water.
> 2. Ask questions about ice to encourage children to share observations.
> 3. Have children take their ice to water and play.

Making a Home for Penguins
> 1. Tell children that some penguins live on ice.
> 2. Show them ice in milk carton. Encourage children to comment on shape of ice. Put ice in water.

Here Come the Penguins and Fish
> 1. Give each child a cork (penguin) to play with on ice and in water, then add a toy fish to the water.
> 2. Encourage children to talk about what they did with toy penguins, fish, ice, and water.
> 3. Ask if they would like to live in a home of ice and water and what they would need or do on the ice.

Role-Playing Penguins
> Let the children pretend they are penguins and role play some of the things penguins do.

Session 3: Making Comparisons
Who is Taller, You or the Penguin?
1. Attach Emperor Penguin poster to wall. Explain that emperor penguins are the biggest kind of penguin and the penguin on the poster is same size as real emperor penguin.
2. Have the children estimate how their height compares to that of the emperor penguin.
3. Let the children take turns comparing their height with emperor penguin on the poster.

More Comparisons
1. Trace around each child on paper and let children color tracings.
2. Have children compare tracings with poster.

Extensions for First Graders
1. Have children label body parts on their tracings.
2. Have them use adding machine tape to make a bar graph of their height.

Activity 2: The Emperor Penguin

Session 1: Getting to Know More About Penguins
The Emperor Penguin Poster
1. In front of poster, ask questions to help children remember what they learned about penguins.
2. Have them identify penguin body parts, use of beak, colors.

Feathers
Have children hold feathers and point to places on penguin where they think there are feathers.

Staying Warm
1. For a count of five, have each child hold ice cube in a hand covered with a mitten, glove or sock, and then in their uncovered hand to discover which hand stays warmer.
2. Explain that mittens keep hands warm just like feathers keep penguins warm.
3. Encourage children to think of clothes they wear to keep warm.

Session 2: Making Paper-Bag Penguins
Have children make a child-designed or model penguin.

Session 3: Penguin Families
Playing With Penguins
Let children play with paper penguins on paper ice and paper water.

The Penguin Drama
Present the penguin drama.

Role-Playing Parent Penguins

1. Pretend everyone is a penguin on ice in cold wind. What can they do as penguins to stay warm? Snuggle all the youngsters together.
2. Give each "penguin" a plastic egg (with a paper baby penguin inside) to keep warm. Egg hatches and children play with their baby penguin..

Making Baby Penguins

Have children find baby penguin's body parts, then glue on cotton or stuffing.

Playing with Baby Penguins and Their Parents

1. Let children create own dramas with paper penguins, eggs, paper water, and paper ice.
2. Give each child a paper fish to take home with their penguins.

Comparisons

1. Encourage children to talk about what they see on Baby Emperor Penguin drawing and find the baby's body parts. Compare baby and adult penguins on the two drawings.
2. Show Emperor Penguin Egg drawing. Tell the children the egg is actual size. Have children compare size of egg and baby penguin to their hands, feet, body parts, and other items in the room.

Comparing Penguins with Other Birds

1. Have children compare what penguins and other birds have and do in common.
2. Have them compare penguin poster with live bird or bird pictures.

Going Further

Encourage children to create penguin pictures and stories, make up dramas, and think of penguin activities to do on snow and ice.

Session 4: A Penguin Parent

A Penguin Parent

Dress a child like a penguin parent and have her show group how penguin keeps egg warm. Let other children take turns.

Going Further

Let children balance objects on feet.

Extensions for First Graders

1. Learn about other types of penguins.
2. Using a globe, place stickers where penguins live.
3. Compare animal life in Antarctic and Arctic regions.

Activity 3: Hungry Young Penguins

Session 1: Penguins Eating Fish

Role-Playing Hungry Young Penguins

Let the children pretend they are penguins and eat fish crackers.

Session 2: Hungry Penguins Game

Hungry Penguins Catch Fish
1. Give children paper oceans and cups of fish crackers.
2. Have them pretend they are hungry penguins and add and take away (eat) fish crackers as you tell a story.

Hungry Penguins Game with Toy Fish
1. Let children play game independently using toy fish. Older children may record fish story with equations.
2. Have child close eyes as another child takes some fish away. First child opens eyes and guesses how many were taken away.

Extensions for Kindergartners and First Graders
  'As you tell story, record data of number of fish being eaten by penguins as equations. Have older children record story using equations.

Activity 4: More Fun with Ice

Session 1: Making Ice Shapes
1. Let children play with objects in water, then fill objects with water. Ask children to predict what will happen if objects are filled with water and put in freezer.
2. Put objects in freezer.

Session 2: Ice Shapes
1. Remove objects from freezer and let children gently touch them.
2. Have group try to get ice out of objects.
3. Allow time for ice explorations.

Going Further
1. Let children make ice sculptures. Prepare treat by putting the frozen ice hand in red juice.

Session 3: Ice Investigations
1. Let children find out what happens when they put one ice cube in sun and one in shade, one ice cube in warm water and one in cold.
2. Let them come up with investigations.
3. Ask questions to encourage children to think about process.

Session 4: Making Ice Treats
  Give children cups of fruit juice and pieces of fruit to drop into juice. Ask, "Does fruit sink or float?" Drink juice. Repeat the process, then freeze the juice/fruit mixture.

Session 5: Ice Treats
  Give cups of frozen juice/fruit mixture to children. Let them examine, discuss, and eat it.

Going Further
  Make punch of chunks of frozen juice and fruit.

Assessment Suggestions

Selected Student Outcomes

1. Students gain experience with the concepts of freezing, melting, and floating through their exploration of ice and water.

2. Students are able to compare their own size, shape, and body structures to those of an emperor penguin.

3. Students are able to create a paper model of a penguin and use it to explain penguin feeding, parenting behaviors and locomotion.

4. Students are able to role-play behaviors that help penguins survive in a cold environment.

Built-In Assessment Activities

Ice Play

In Activity 1, Session 2, An Ice Home, students are given their cups of water from the day before that have now frozen in the freezer overnight. Teachers guide an exploration of the ice in and out of a tub of water by asking the following questions.

"What happened to the water in our cups?"
"What does the ice feel like?"
"What does the ice look like?"
"What is happening to the ice now?"
"What is happening to the ice in the water?"

Teachers can observe the spontaneous play and conversation that occurs as children explore. Responses to questions provide information on the degree to which students understand the concepts of freezing, melting, and floating.
(Outcome 1)

As Tall as a Penguin!

In Activity 1, Session 3, Making Comparisons, students are shown a full-size emperor penguin poster. In kindergarten, the teacher asks, "Do you think you are taller or shorter than the emperor penguin?" The teacher can listen to their guesses and observe their responses when they come up to the poster to measure themselves. Students can compare their height, size, and body structures to the penguin, as teachers again note verbal and physical responses to questions.
(Outcome 2)

The Penguin Dramas

In Activity 2, Session 2, Making Paper-Bag Penguins and Session 3, Penguin Families, students make a model of a penguin, listen and participate in a drama enacted by the teacher, and use the paper-bag penguins in a variety of real-penguin life dramas. As students create their own dramas, the teacher can watch for feeding, parenting, locomotion, and keeping-warm behaviors. The spontaneous dramas will also evoke new vocabulary and language usage.
(Outcome 3)

I'm a Penguin

In Activity 2, Session 3, Penguin Families and Session 4, A Penguin Parent, students role play being part of a penguin family on an icy shore. They later dress-up as penguins using a dark jacket and pillow. The teacher can observe the behaviors of the student "penguins," including whether the behavior includes keeping warm in a cold environment.
(Outcome 4)

Additional Assessment Ideas

Penguin Ice Festival

Later in the year, conduct an ice fair or festival that uses all of the ice activities from the unit. Observe students' responses to the activities again, and look for their usage of new language that explains ice and water concepts.
(Outcome 1)

Penguins at Home

Send the paper-bag penguins, eggs, poster, and other props home with the students. Ask families to watch and listen to the dramas and role plays, and describe what was presented in a note back to the teacher.
(Outcomes 2, 3, 4)

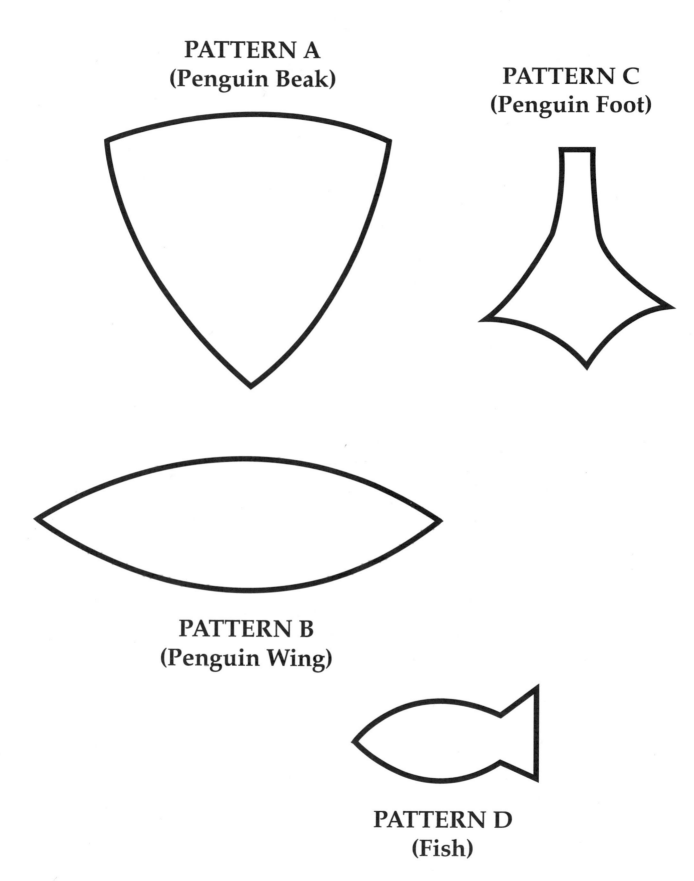

PATTERN A
(Penguin Beak)

PATTERN C
(Penguin Foot)

PATTERN B
(Penguin Wing)

PATTERN D
(Fish)

Cut two of each pattern (except the fish) when making a Paper-Bag Penguin.

Paper-Bag Penguin Patterns

Emperor Penguin Egg

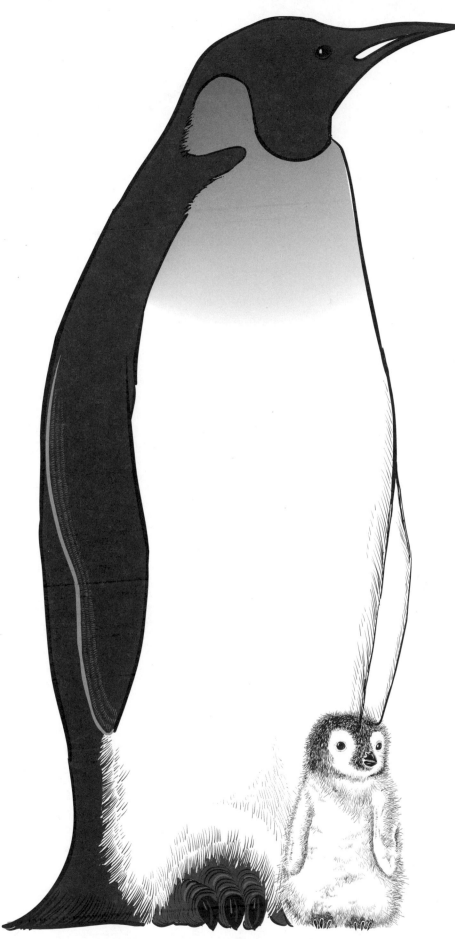

© 1995 by The Regents of the University of California
LHS GEMS—*Penguins And Their Young*

Emperor Penguin and Baby

Baby Emperor Penguin

Baby Penguins Activity Sheet

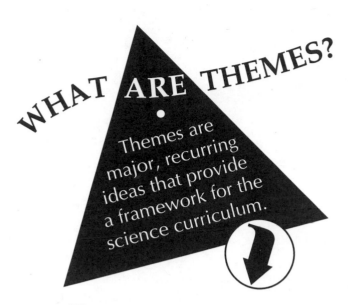

WHAT ARE THEMES?

Themes are major, recurring ideas that provide a framework for the science curriculum.

The word "themes" is used in many different ways in our daily lives and in educational circles. In the GEMS series, themes are key recurring ideas that cut across all the scientific disciplines. Themes are bigger than facts, concepts, or theories. They link various theories from many disciplines. They also have been described as "the sap that runs through the curriculum," in the sense that they permeate through and arise from the curriculum. By listing the themes that run through a particular GEMS unit on the title page, you can see how the unit fits into the "big picture" of science and connects to other GEMS units. The theme "Patterns of Change," for example, suggests that the unit or some important part of it exemplifies larger scientific ideas about why, how, and in what ways change takes place, whether it is a chemical reaction or a caterpillar becoming a butterfly. GEMS has selected ten major themes:

Systems and Interactions   Scale
Models and Simulations   Structure
Stability   Energy
Patterns of Change   Matter
Evolution   Diversity and Unity

If you are interested in investigating themes and the thematic approach to teaching and constructing curriculum, write or call for our handbook, *To Build A House: GEMS and the Thematic Approach to Teaching Science.* For more information about all of our GEMS guides and an order brochure, write or call:

GEMS
Lawrence Hall of Science
University of California
Berkeley, CA 94720-5200

(510) 642-7771
(510) 643-0309 (fax)

Thanks for your interest in GEMS!

GEMS Guides

Please contact GEMS for a descriptive brochure and ordering information
— GEMS student data sheets are now available in Spanish —

TEACHER'S GUIDES

Acid Rain
Grades 6–10

Animal Defenses
Preschool–K

Animals in Action
Grades 5–9

Ant Homes Under The Ground
Preschool–1

Bubble Festival
Grades K–6

Bubble-ology
Grades 5–9

Build It! Festival
Grades K–6

Buzzing A Hive
Grades K–3

Chemical Reactions
Grades 6–10

Color Analyzers
Grades 5–9

Convection: A Current Event
Grades 6–9

Crime Lab Chemistry
Grades 4–8

Discovering Density
Grades 6–10

Earth, Moon, and Stars
Grades 5–9

Earthworms
Grades 6–10

Experimenting with Model Rockets
Grades 6–10

Fingerprinting
Grades 4–8

Frog Math: Predict, Ponder, Play
Grades K–3

Global Warming
Grades 7–10

Group Solutions
Grades K–4

Height-O-Meters
Grades 6–10

Hide A Butterfly
Preschool–K

Hot Water and Warm Homes
Grades 4–8

In All Probability
Grades 3–6

Investigating Artifacts
Grades K–6

Involving Dissolving
Grades 1–3

Ladybugs
Preschool–1

Learning About Learning
Grades 6–8

Liquid Explorations
Grades 1–3

Mapping Animal Movements
Grades 5–9

Mapping Fish Habitats
Grades 6–10

Math Around the World
Grades 5–8

Moons of Jupiter
Grades 4–9

More Than Magnifiers
Grades 6–9

Mystery Festival
Grades 2–8

Of Cabbages and Chemistry
Grades 4–8

Oobleck: What Do Scientists Do?
Grades 4–8

Paper Towel Testing
Grades 5–9

Penguins And Their Young
Preschool–1

QUADICE
Grades 4–8

River Cutters
Grades 6–9

Secret Formulas
Grades 1–3

Stories in Stone
Grades 4–9

Terrarium Habitats
Grades K–6

Tree Homes
Preschool–1

Vitamin C Testing
Grades 4–8

ASSEMBLY PRESENTER'S GUIDES

The "Magic" of Electricity
Grades 3–6

Solids, Liquids, and Gases
Grades 3–6

EXHIBIT GUIDES

Shapes, Loops & Images
All ages

The Wizard's Lab
All ages

HANDBOOKS

GEMS Teacher's Handbook

GEMS Leader's Handbook

Insights & Outcomes
(Assessment)

Once Upon A GEMS Guide
(Literature Connections)

A Parent's Guide to GEMS

To Build A House
(Thematic Approach
to Teaching Science)

Write, Call, or Fax:

GEMS
Lawrence Hall of Science
University of California
Berkeley, CA 94720-5200

(510) 642-7771
fax: (510) 643-0309